FOR THE LOVE OF
oats

Amy Ruth Finegold

photography by Clare Winfield

FOR THE LOVE OF
oats

delicious recipes
for healthy
breakfasts, snacks,
bakes and drinks

RYLAND PETERS & SMALL
LONDON • NEW YORK

To my husband Todd, my son Jake and my baby girl in my belly who kept me very hungry during the writing of this book.

Senior Designer Sonya Nathoo
Commissioning Editor Stephanie Milner
Head of Production Patricia Harrington
Art Director Leslie Harrington
Editorial Director Julia Charles

Prop Stylist Polly Webb-Wilson
Food Stylist Rosie Reynolds
Indexer Hilary Bird

First published in 2014
by Ryland Peters & Small,
20–21 Jockey's Fields,
London WC1R 4BW
and
519 Broadway, 5th Floor,
New York NY 10012
www.rylandpeters.com

10 9 8 7 6 5 4 3 2 1

Printed and bound in China

Text © Amy Ruth Finegold 2014
Design and photographs © Ryland Peters & Small 2014

ISBN: 978-1-84975-556-6

A CIP record for this book is available from the British Library. US Library of Congress cataloging-in-publication data has been applied for.

Note

• Both British (Metric) and American (Imperial plus US cups) are included in these recipes for your convenience, however it is important to work with one set of measurements and not alternate between the two within a recipe.
• All spoon measurements are level unless specified.
• All eggs are medium (UK) or large (US), unless specified as large, in which case US extra-large should be used. Uncooked or partially cooked eggs should not be served to the very old, frail, young children, pregnant women or those with compromised immune systems.
• Ovens should be preheated to the specified temperatures. We recommend using an oven thermometer. If using a fan-assisted oven, adjust temperatures according to the manufacturer's instructions.
• All the recipes within this book can be made using dairy, almond or soy milk.
• Plain/all-purpose flour can be substituted with gluten-free plain/all-purpose flour if following a gluten-free diet but the recipe will need to introduce xanthan gum to achieve a similar result.

contents

introduction

Ever since first learning about the importance of eating a healthy diet, I have made sure that I always start my day with a wholesome meal. It is well understood by nutritionists that eating well at the beginning of each day is key to getting your metabolism going, but I also find that a good breakfast can give me consistent energy throughout the day. People often ask me, 'what's the best food we can eat in the morning?' The answer is, of course, quite simply, oats – the star of this book!

From a nutritional standpoint, the low glycemic index (GI) of oats supports our wellbeing by slowly raising our blood sugar and then providing a steady stream of energy. This keeps us feeling fuller for longer, curbs appetite and improves our concentration so we can function at our best. One bowl of oatmeal or porridge in the morning has the perfect amount of calories to keep us energized, while priming our bodies for healthy weight control.

Oats also offer a better nutritional profile than wholegrain wheat and are considered a 'super grain', high in manganese and vitamin B1, with a generous amount of protein and fibre thrown in for good measure. The fibre found in oats is particularly impressive, since they contain both soluble and insoluble fibre. The soluble fibre is called beta-glucan, which helps reduce the bad kind of cholesterol, known as low-density lipoprotein (LDL), while the insoluble fibre is very important for healthy digestion.

Oats can also be a useful food for those on a wheat-free diet and certified gluten-free brands are now readily available (although not all those intolerant to gluten are able to enjoy them so it's best to check before serving to others). If you wish to convert a recipe in this book that uses wheat flour to a gluten-free one, simply substitute a gluten-free plain/all-purpose flour and add a little xanthan gum, as specified in the recipe.

Oats come in many different forms, including old-fashioned and quick-cook rolled oats, steel-cut oats and oat groats. They can also be ground into a flour for baking, which makes a tasty and nutritious alternative to wheat flours. The recipes here feature all these types of oats and show just how easily they can be prepared and enjoyed in a variety of delicious ways.

Although I have specified my own preference within each recipe, all of the recipes in this book can be made using dairy, almond or soy milk as preferred, or you can go all out with homemade oat milk, made by steeping oats in water to extract their goodness (see page 61).

Liquid sweeteners are used for most recipes too. I use honey and brown rice syrup for granola bars because they are the best 'binder' for these recipes but I prefer the taste of maple syrup so I use this to sweeten oatmeal and porridge. Agave syrup is another great multi-purpose sweetener without a distinctive taste whereas coconut nectar or syrup has a stronger flavour as well as a lower GI than other sweeteners.

Choose one of my easy-to-make oatmeal, muesli and granolas for breakfast or make the bars, cookies or muffins for a healthy snack on the go and enjoy them, for the love of oats!

oatmeal
and porridge

Peaches and cream reminds me of the perfect summer breakfast, one that you can replicate all year round using peach preserves in place of fresh peaches. Creamy, sweet and indulgent you'll make this oatmeal again and again.

peaches and cream oatmeal

240 ml/1 cup whole milk
1 teaspoon pure vanilla extract
200 g/2 cups old-fashioned or quick-cook rolled oats
50 g/$\frac{1}{2}$ cup flaked/slivered almonds
2–3 peaches, stoned/pitted and sliced (or 70 g/$\frac{1}{4}$ cup peach preserve)
1 tablespoon butter
2 tablespoons brown sugar
crème fraîche, to garnish

a sterilized glass jar with airtight lid (optional)

Serves 4

Begin by combining 650 ml/2$\frac{3}{4}$ cups of water with the milk and pure vanilla extract in a saucepan or pot set over a low–medium heat. Bring to a simmer then add the oats and bring to a boil. Quickly turn down the heat and simmer for 15–20 minutes, or 5 minutes if using quick-cook oats, stirring occasionally.

Meanwhile prepare the almonds. Put the almonds in a dry pan/skillet set over a low–medium heat. Toast for 5 minutes or until the almonds are golden brown. Remove from the heat and set aside.

Now prepare the peaches. Place the fruit slices in a frying pan/skillet set over a medium heat with the butter and sugar. Sauté for 5–7 minutes or until the peaches become soft.

Put the toasted almonds and prepared peaches in a mixing bowl, reserving a small amount of each for the topping, and stir to combine. Stir into the cooked oatmeal.

Pour into bowls and garnish with a slice of the reserved peach and a dollop of crème fraîche. Sprinkle extra toasted almonds on each dish for added crunch.

Note
You can store the toasted almonds in a sterilized glass jar sealed with an airtight lid for up to 2 weeks.

If peaches aren't in season you could substitute them with peach preserve which is just as delicious and makes this dish quicker to prepare.

100 g/1 cup steel-cut oats
125 ml/$\frac{1}{2}$ cup milk
1 teaspoon pure vanilla
  extract
a pinch of salt
50 g/$\frac{1}{2}$ cup mixed fresh
  blueberries, raspberries
  and blackcurrants
4 tablespoons maple syrup,
  to serve

Serves 4

Steel-cut oats have a rougher texture than old-fashioned rolled oats which is surprisingly pleasant on the palate. They take a longer time to cook but are well worth the time spent by the stove. I like to eat this dish on a cold morning when I want an extra-hearty start to the day.

steel-cut berry oatmeal

Place 800 ml/3$\frac{1}{4}$ cups of water in a medium saucepan or pot set over a high heat and bring to a boil. Add the oats once the water is bubbling and keep on the heat. Bring the oats and water back to a boil then turn the heat down and continue to cook for 20 minutes with the lid on but with air escaping. Stir the mixture occasionally so nothing sticks on the bottom.

Add the milk, vanilla and a pinch of salt to the pan and simmer for a further 10 minutes. Finally, add the fruit and simmer for 5 minutes longer so the fruit is hot but still retains its shape.

Pour the oatmeal into bowls and drizzle each with a tablespoon of maple syrup before serving.

A note on steel-cut oats
These are oat groats that have been chopped into small pieces. These are sometimes referred to as Irish oats.

Nothing beats your morning coffee so here I bring your favourite cup of Joe to the breakfast table. If you own an espresso machine, you most likely have a milk frother, which adds the finishing touch to this indulgent dish.

mochaccino oatmeal

480 ml/2 cups milk

2 tablespoons cocoa powder, plus extra for dusting

200 g/2 cups old-fashioned or quick-cook rolled oats

3 tablespoons brewed espresso coffee

2 tablespoons maple syrup

60 ml/^{1}/4 cup milk foam, to garnish

an espresso machine fitted with a foam attachment (optional)

Serves 4

Combine 420 ml/1^3/4 cups of water with the milk and cocoa powder in a saucepan or pot set over a medium heat. Bring to a simmer then add the oats and turn the heat up to bring the mixture to a boil. Once bubbling, quickly turn down the heat and simmer for 15–20 minutes, or 5 minutes if using quick-cook oats, stirring occasionally.

Remove the pan from the heat and stir in the espresso and maple syrup.

Make a milk foam, following the instructions on your espresso machine if you have one, or by scalding the milk in a saucepan or pot set over a very high heat.

Pour the oatmeal into bowls and top with a dollop of milk foam. Dust with cocoa powder and serve.

My favourite thing about oatmeal is how easily it can be transformed into a comforting dessert. Sautéed apples with honey in a warm bowl of oatmeal is close enough to apple pie for me!

apple pie oatmeal

2 apples, sliced
1 tablespoon butter
4 teaspoons ground
   cinnamon
250 ml/1 cup almond milk
200 g/2 cups old-fashioned
   or quick-cook rolled oats
2 tablespoons honey, plus
   extra to serve
25 g/^{1}/4 cup chopped walnuts,
   to garnish
2 tablespoons plain yogurt
   (optional), to serve

Serves 4

Sauté the sliced apples with the butter and cinnamon in a medium frying pan/skillet set over a medium–high heat. Cook for about 5 minutes until the sliced fruit is soft on the outside but still a little firm on the inside. Remove from the pan and set aside.

Combine 700 ml/2^3/4 cups of water with the almond milk in a saucepan or pot set over a medium heat and bring to a simmer.

Add the oats and bring to a boil. Once bubbling, quickly turn down the heat and simmer for 15–20 minutes, or 5 minutes if using quick-cook oats, stirring occasionally. After 15 minutes, pour in half of the apple mixture and continue to cook for the last 5 minutes. Remove from the heat and stir in the honey.

Pour the oatmeal into bowls, garnish with chopped walnuts and top with the remaining apples and extra honey to taste. For extra creaminess you can serve with plain yogurt on the side.

A note on rolled oats
Old-fashioned rolled oats are are flakes from the groat that have been rolled. Quick-cook rolled oats are the same as old-fashioned rolled oats, but they have been rolled thinner, so the cooking time is less.

Oatmeal is most often cooked on the stove, but following the oven method here makes a great change and takes oatmeal to a new dimension. When baking oatmeal, I always add an egg which changes its consistency nicely.

baked fruit and nut oatmeal

200 g/2 cups old-fashioned
  rolled oats
20 g/¼ cup chopped
  almonds
1 teaspoon ground cinnamon
55 g/¼ cup brown sugar or
  ½ tablespoon stevia
550 ml/2¼ cups milk
1 teaspoon pure vanilla
  extract
2 tablespoons melted butter,
  plus extra for greasing
1 egg
70 g/1 cup frozen blueberries

*a round 15-cm/6-in baking dish,
  greased*

Serves 6

Preheat oven to 180°C (350°F) Gas 4.

Mix the oats, almonds, cinnamon and sugar of your choice together in a large mixing bowl. In a separate bowl, mix the milk, vanilla, melted butter and egg together.

Pour the wet mixture into the dry ingredients and stir to combine. Fold in the blueberries then transfer the oatmeal to the prepared baking dish.

Bake in the preheated oven for 30–45 minutes, until the edges are crisp and golden.

Set aside to cool slightly before serving.

190 g/1 cup oat groats
2 bananas, mashed, plus
    1 sliced to garnish
1 teaspoon ground cinnamon,
    plus extra to serve
4 tablespoons almond milk
8 teaspoons maple syrup,
    to serve

Serves 4

This is a recipe for the oat purist. Oat groats are the most unrefined and unprocessed oats so they are the highest in nutritional value. It is best to soak these oats overnight before cooking so be sure to leave plenty of time to prepare this power-house cereal.

banana oat groat cereal

Soak the oat groats in 720 ml/3 cups of water in a saucepan or pot overnight.

In the morning, bring the pan to a boil, then cook on a low heat with the lid off for 30 minutes. The water should evaporate, leaving you with a mushy, rice-like consistency.

Add the mashed banana and cinnamon to the pan and stir it until the banana is mixed through and the oatmeal piping hot.

Pour into bowls and top each with a few slices of banana. Add a tablespoon of almond milk and 2 teaspoons of maple syrup to each bowl, sprinkle with ground cinnamon and serve.

A note on oat groats
Oat groats are the whole oat kernel with just the husk removed. It needs the most amount of cooking time and it's best to soak these grains before they are cooked.

Quinoa is a super healthy and popular grain that makes a great warm breakfast. By mixing oats and quinoa you get the nutritional bonus of them both. The smooth texture of the oatmeal goes well with the cooked pearls of quinoa.

quinoa oatmeal

500 ml/2 cups almond milk
50 g/^{1}/$_2$ cup old-fashioned
    rolled oats
50 g/^{1}/$_2$ cup dry quinoa
1 teaspoon cinnamon
^{1}/$_2$ teaspoon pure vanilla
    extract
2 tablespoons maple syrup,
    plus extra to serve
1 banana, sliced
50 g/^{1}/$_2$ cup mixed fresh
    berries

Serves 2

Bring the milk to a boil in a medium saucepan or pot set over a medium–high heat.

Add the oats and quinoa and bring to a boil again. Once bubbling, reduce the heat and add the cinnamon and vanilla. Simmer with the lid on for 20 minutes then pour in the maple syrup and stir well.

Divide the oatmeal between two bowls. Top each with sliced banana and fresh berries and drizzle over extra maple syrup to taste.

This oatmeal is the perfect autumn/fall bowlful. Combining pumpkin purée and pie spices makes for a warming treat!

pumpkin pie oatmeal

900 ml/3 $^1/_2$ cups almond milk
1 teaspoon ground cinnamon
$^1/_8$ teaspoon ground nutmeg
$^1/_8$ teaspoon ground ginger
$^1/_8$ teaspoon ground cloves
160 g/$^3/_4$ cup pumpkin purée
  from a can
200 g/2 cups old-fashioned
  or quick-cook rolled oats
40 g/$^1/_4$ cup (dark) raisins
3 tablespoons maple syrup

Garnish
20 g/$^1/_8$ cup pumpkin seeds
15 g/$^1/_8$ cup pecans

*a sterilized glass jar with
  airtight lid (optional)*

Serves 4

Put the milk, spices and pumpkin purée in a saucepan or pot set over a gentle heat and bring to a simmer.

Add the oats to the pan and bring to a boil. Quickly turn down the heat and simmer for 15–20 minutes, or 5 minutes for quick-cook oats, stirring occasionally. Add the raisins for the last minute of cooking time and stir so they become plump and warm.

Meanwhile, prepare the pecan and pumpkin seed garnish. Put the pumpkin seeds and pecans in a dry frying pan/skillet set over a low–medium heat. Toast for 5 minutes then remove from the pan and set aside.

When the oatmeal is ready, remove the pan from the heat and add the maple syrup. Mix well then pour into bowls to serve.

Garnish with the toasted pumpkin seeds and pecans and enjoy.

Note
You can store the toasted seeds and nuts in a sterilized glass jar sealed with an airtight lid for up to 2 weeks.

Seeds are the healthiest plant-based food – full of minerals and protein, we should all find ways of eating more. Here is an easy way to incorporate them into your everyday bowl of oats.

super-seeded oatmeal

250 ml/1 cup almond milk
200 g/2 cups old-fashioned
  or quick-cook rolled oats
15 g/^{1}/8 cup milled chia seeds
  or flaxseeds
15 g/^{1}/8 cup hemp seeds
25 g/^{1}/4 cup chopped dates
15 g/^{1}/8 cup sunflower seeds
2 tablespoons maple syrup,
  plus extra to taste

Serves 4

Combine 700 ml/2^3/4 cups of water with the milk in a saucepan or pot set over a medium heat. Bring to a simmer, then add the oats. Stir and bring to a boil. Quickly turn down the heat and simmer for 15–20 minutes, or for 5 minutes if using quick-cook oats, stirring occasionally.

Remove the pan from the heat and add the chia seeds or flaxseeds, hemp seeds, and chopped dates. Mix well.

Pour the seeded oatmeal into bowls, sprinkle with sunflower seeds and drizzle with maple syrup to taste.

muesli
and granola

One way to differentiate between muesli and granola is that muesli isn't usually toasted. Muesli is traditionally made by soaking uncooked oats with milk, yogurt or juice. However, here I toast the sunflower seeds and oats to enhance the flavour of the dish.

date and sunflower muesli

60 g/^{2}/3 cup old-fashioned
  rolled oats
40 g/^{1}/4 cup sunflower seeds,
  1 teaspoon reserved
  to garnish
300 ml/1 ^{1}/4 cups milk
125 g/^{1}/2 cup plain yogurt
1 teaspoon ground cinnamon
1 tablespoon flaxseeds
^{1}/2 teaspoon pure vanilla
  extract
1 tablespoon honey
30 g/^{1}/4 cup chopped dates,
  1 teaspoon reserved
  to garnish

To serve
1 orange, peeled and sliced
the seeds of ^{1}/2 a
  pomegranate

*a baking sheet, greased and
  lined with baking parchment*

*a sterilized glass jar with
  airtight lid (optional)*

Serves 2

Preheat the oven to 180°C (350°F) Gas 4.

Scatter the oats and sunflower seeds on the prepared baking sheet and bake in the preheated oven for 10 minutes, until light brown. Remove the toasted oats and seeds and set aside to cool.

Put the remaining ingredients in a large mixing bowl and stir. Add the cooled oats and seeds and mix well. Take care to fully incorporate the milk with the yogurt. Cover and leave the oats to soak in the fridge overnight.

When ready to serve, stir the muesli and pour into bowls. Garnish with the reserved chopped date and a handful of toasted sunflower seeds. For an extra burst of citrus add orange slices and pomegranate seeds to the muesli before serving.

Note
You can store the toasted oats and seeds in a sterilized glass jar sealed with an airtight lid for up to 2 weeks.

The addition of chia seeds to this bircher muesli takes it to a new nutritional level. The texture of the rolled oats and soaked cherries blends beautifully for a delicious and nutritious breakfast. Running to the office? Take it on the go.

cherry chia muesli

60 g/²/₃ cup old-fashioned rolled oats
1 tablespoon chia seeds
30 g/¹/₄ cup dried cherries
375 ml/1 ¹/₂ cups milk
¹/₂ teaspoon pure vanilla extract
1 apple, chopped into matchsticks or grated
10 g/¹/₈ cup flaked/slivered almonds
1 tablespoon honey

a sterilized glass jar with airtight lid (optional)

Serves 2

Mix the oats, chia seeds, cherries, milk and vanilla together in a large mixing bowl. Cover and leave to soak in the fridge overnight.

When ready to serve, stir well and pour into bowls. Add the grated apple and almonds and drizzle with honey.

If you don't use all of the chia muesli you can store it in an airtight glass jar for up to 2 days, or take it on the go in a chill bag to eat later in the day.

Variation
Sliced pear and dried prunes are delicious alternatives to the sliced apple and dried cherries used here.

Granola isn't just for breakfast. I put it in a resealable bag and have a snack to hand for either me or my son. Cranberries and pecans are both a visually appealing and tasty addition to this granola recipe.

cranberry pecan granola

200 g/2 cups old-fashioned or quick-cook rolled oats
200 g/1 cup chopped pecans
30 g/^{1}/3 cup unsweetened shredded/dessicated coconut
1 tablespoon ground cinnamon
75 g/^{1}/2 cup dried cranberries
2 tablespoons vegetable oil
60 ml/^{1}/4 cup maple syrup

To serve
plain yogurt
mixed fresh berries (sliced strawberries, raspberries and blueberries all work well)

a large baking sheet, coated in oil or baking spray

a sterilized glass jar with airtight lid (optional)

Serves 4

Preheat the oven to 140°C (275°F) Gas 1.

Mix the oats, pecans, coconut, cinnamon and cranberries together in a large mixing bowl. Add the oil and maple syrup and mix well using your hands to ensure that the oat mixture is well covered with oil and syrup.

Pour the granola mixture onto the prepared baking sheet and spread out. Bake in the preheated oven for 40 minutes, stirring every 10–15 minutes so that the oats don't burn.

Remove from the oven and set aside to cool before serving with yogurt and mixed fresh berries.

Note
You can store the granola in a sterilized glass jar sealed with an airtight lid set in the fridge for up to 2 weeks.

A parfait is the most elegant way to pair oats, yogurt and fruit. Choose a martini glass to serve it for someone special or a tall ice cream float glass for kids. There's a lot of freedom in its assembly too. If you love it creamy, make a thick layer of yogurt and if you want it crunchy, pile on the granola.

yogurt granola parfait

For the granola
200 g/2 cups old-fashioned
   rolled oats
60 g/^{3}/4 cup chopped
   almonds
25 g/^{1}/4 cup flaxseeds
30 ml/^{1}/8 cup maple syrup
3 tablespoons vegetable oil
3 tablespoons brown sugar
150 g/1 cup (dark) raisins

For the parfait
3 tablespoons honey, plus
   extra to serve
1 teaspoon ground cinnamon
430 g/2 cups Greek yogurt
125 g/1 cup mixed berries

*a large baking sheet, coated
   in oil or baking spray*

*a sterilized glass jar with
   airtight lid (optional)*

2–4 glass bowls

Serves 2–4

Preheat oven to 140°C (275°F) Gas 1.

Put all of the granola ingredients except the raisins in a large mixing bowl and mix well so everything is well-coated in oil and syrup. Spread the mixture onto the prepared baking sheet and bake in the preheated oven for 40 minutes, or until golden brown, stirring every 10 minutes.

Remove the granola from the oven and place the baking sheet on a wire rack to cool.

Once cool, put the granola in a large mixing bowl and add the raisins. Take out 180 g/1 1/2 cups for the parfait recipe and store the rest in a sterilized glass jar with an airtight lid.

To make the parfait, mix 2 tablespoons of honey and the cinnamon with the yogurt. In a separate bowl, mix the remaining tablespoon of honey with the berries. Put a layer of the yogurt into each glass bowl. Smooth the top, then add a layer of granola, followed by a layer of mixed berries. Repeat until you have used all of the ingredients. Dust with cinnamon and add extra honey if you have a sweet tooth!

Note
You can store the granola in a sterilized glass jar sealed with an airtight lid set in the fridge for up to 2 weeks.

This granola uses coconut in all its forms. From coconut sugar, to coconut oil and of course, shredded/dessicated coconut, it satisfies the strongest coconut cravings.

coconut flax granola

200 g/2 cup old-fashioned
   or quick-cook rolled oats
40 g/^{1}/2 cup chopped
   almonds
25 g/^{1}/4 cup chopped walnuts
25 g/^{1}/4 cup milled flaxseeds
70 g/^{3}/4 cup unsweetened
   shredded/dessicated
   coconut
30 ml/^{1}/8 cup maple syrup
3 tablespoons melted
   coconut oil
3 tablespoons coconut sugar
150 g/1 cup (dark) raisins

To serve
tropical fruit such as
   pineapple and mango,
   chopped
plain yogurt

*a large baking sheet, coated
   in oil or baking spray*

*a sterilized glass jar with
   airtight lid (optional)*

Serves 4

Preheat oven to 140°C (275°F) Gas 1.

Put all of the ingredients except the raisins in a large mixing bowl and mix well so everything is well-coated in oil and syrup. Spread the mixture onto the prepared baking sheet and bake in the preheated oven for 40 minutes, or until golden brown, stirring every 10 minutes.

Remove the granola from the oven and place the baking sheet on a wire rack to cool.

Once cool, put the granola in a large mixing bowl and add the raisins. Serve with pieces of tropical fruit and yogurt.

Note
You can store the granola in a sterilized glass jar sealed with an airtight lid set in the fridge for up to 2 weeks.

Vanilla and almonds are a natural flavour pairing with sweet and warm nutty notes. I love mixing chopped and whole almonds to add a variety of textures to this cereal.

vanilla almond granola

200 g/2 cups old-fashioned rolled oats
60 g/^{3}/4 cup chopped almonds
25 g/^{1}/4 cup whole almonds
25 g/^{1}/4 cup of wheatgerm (or rice bran if following gluten-free diet)
25 g/^{1}/4 cup milled flaxseeds
3 tablespoons melted coconut oil
30 ml/^{1}/8 cup maple syrup
2 teaspoons pure vanilla extract

3 tablespoons brown sugar

a large baking sheet, coated in oil or baking spray

a sterilized glass jar with airtight lid (optional)

Serves 4

Preheat oven to 140°C (275°F) Gas 1.

Put all of the ingredients in a large mixing bowl and mix well so everything is well-coated in oil and syrup. Spread the mixture onto the prepared baking sheet and bake in the preheated oven for 40 minutes, or until golden brown, stirring every 10 minutes.

Remove the granola from the oven and place the baking sheet on a wire rack to cool before serving.

Note
You can store the granola in a sterilized glass jar sealed with an airtight lid set in the fridge for up to 2 weeks.

bars and cookies

Granola bars are a versatile snack or breakfast. Whether for the kids' school bags or a pre-workout snack, they are portable and healthy. The possibilities are endless with the kind of nuts or dried fruit to add. Swap the chocolate chips for raisins to please a young palate!

almond oat granola bars

200 g/2 cups old-fashioned rolled oats
80 g/1 cup chopped almonds
140 ml/$^1/_2$ cup plus 1 tablespoon honey
25 g/$^1/_8$ cup dark brown sugar
50 g/$^1/_4$ cup almond butter
1 teaspoon pure vanilla extract
70 g/$^1/_2$ cup (dark) raisins
40 g/1$^1/_2$ cups crisped rice cereal
50 g/$^1/_2$ cup milled flaxseeds
a pinch of salt
1 egg plus 1 egg white, whisked

an 18 x 28-cm/7 x 11-in baking pan, greased and lined with baking parchment

Makes 12

Preheat the oven to 180°C (350°F) Gas 4.

Pulse the oats in a food processor, then transfer to a large mixing bowl and add the almonds. Stir well, then pour the oat mixture onto the prepared baking sheet. Toast in the preheated oven for 15 minutes, or until golden brown. Remove from the oven and set aside to cool, reducing the heat of the oven to 150°C (300°F) Gas 2.

Melt the honey, sugar, almond butter and vanilla in a small saucepan or pot set over a medium heat. Bring the mixture to a boil and then quickly turn down the heat and simmer for a few minutes. Remove from heat and set aside to cool slightly.

Return the cooled toasted oat mixture to the mixing bowl and add the raisins. Then add the crisped rice cereal, flaxseeds and a pinch of salt. Toss to mix everything together. Then, add the honey mixture. Mix together, then add the whisked egg and egg white. Make sure everything is evenly mixed.

Press the mixture into the prepared pan with a flat spatula or the back of a wooden spoon until it is even and firm. Bake for 30 minutes. Remove the baked granola bars from the oven and cool completely before cutting into even bars.

This is a great afternoon treat that showcases apricots. I like chopping Turkish dried apricots for this because their meaty consistency makes for a great bite!

apricot flax oat bars

150 g/1 1/2 cups old-fashioned rolled oats

60 g/1/2 cup chopped walnuts

65 g/1/2 cup plain/all-purpose flour (plus 1/2 teaspoon xanthan gum if using gluten-free plain/all-purpose flour)

170 g/1/2 cup brown rice syrup

25 g/1/8 cup dark brown sugar

100 ml/1/3 cup melted butter

1 teaspoon pure vanilla extract

100 g/1/2 cup chopped apricots

25 g/1/4 cup milled flaxseeds

a pinch of salt

1 egg, whisked

150 g/1/2 cup apricot preserve

an 18 x 28-cm/7 x 11-in baking pan, greased and lined with baking parchment

Makes 12

Preheat the oven to 150°C (300°F) Gas 2.

Pulse the oats in a food processor, then put them in a large mixing bowl with the chopped walnuts and flour. Stir well, then pour the oat mixture onto the prepared baking sheet. Toast in the preheated oven for 15 minutes, or until golden brown. Remove from the oven and set aside to cool, reducing the heat of the oven to 150°C (300°F) Gas 2.

Melt the rice syrup, sugar, butter, xanthan gum (if using) and vanilla in a small saucepan or pot set over a medium heat. Bring the mixture to a boil and then quickly turn down the heat and simmer for a few minutes. Remove from the heat and set aside to cool slightly.

Return the cooled toasted oat mixture to the mixing bowl and add the chopped apricots, flaxseeds and a pinch of salt to the bowl. Toss to mix everything together. Then, add the honey mixture. Mix together, then add the whisked egg. Make sure everything is mixed evenly.

Press down half the mixture in the prepared pan with a flat spatula or back of a wooden spoon until it is even and firmly packed. Then spread a layer of apricot preserve across the oat mixture and finally, spread the remaining of the oat mixture on top.

Bake in the preheated oven for 30 minutes. Remove from the oven and cool completely before cutting into even bars.

I'm always thankful of a 'shortcut' when cooking and working around a busy schedule. Because the granola is pre-made here, this tasty tray just requires assembly and patience while the bars stick together!

ginger cashew 'shortcut' granola bars

200 g/1^3/$_4$ cups Granola
(see page 32) or any plain
granola
60 g/^{1}/$_2$ cup well-chopped
cashews
40 g/^{1}/$_4$ cup well-chopped
crystallized ginger
80 g/1 cup crisped rice cereal
50 g/^{1}/$_4$ cup almond butter
115 g/^{1}/$_3$ cup brown rice
syrup
1 tablespoon vegetable oil

a 20-cm/8-in square baking
pan, greased and lined with
baking parchment

Makes 12

Mix the coconut granola, cashews, ginger and crisped rice cereal together in a large mixing bowl. Add the almond butter, rice syrup and oil and mix well so everything is well-coated.

Press the sticky batter into the pan and set in the fridge to set for at least 3 hours.

Remove from the fridge and cut into even bars before serving.

Variation
Candied citrus peel is a great alternative to crystallized ginger in this recipe and gives the bars a tropical burst of tangy citrus flavour.

Energy and protein bars are everywhere you look and it's easy to understand why. They are the perfect snack for when you're on the go and need to curb hunger pangs. I make these with unsweetened cocoa powder for a chocolate fix and almonds for added protein.

cocoa energy bars

75 g/^{1}/2 cup sliced figs
150 g/1 ^{1}/2 cup old-fashioned rolled oats
35 g/^{1}/4 cup oat flour
25 g/^{1}/3 cups chopped almonds
120 g/1 ^{1}/2 cups crisped rice cereal
50 g/^{1}/3 cup dark/bittersweet chocolate chips
3 tablespoons brown sugar
4 tablespoons cocoa powder
50 g/^{1}/4 cup almond butter

60 ml/^{1}/4 cup coconut oil
115 g/^{1}/3 cup brown rice syrup
80 ml/^{1}/3 cup almond milk
1 teaspoon pure vanilla extract

an 18 x 28-cm/7 x 11-in baking pan, greased and lined with baking parchment

Makes 12

Preheat the oven to 180°C (350°F) Gas 4.

Pulse the figs and oats together in a food processor and transfer the mixture to a large mixing bowl. Add the flour, almonds, crisped rice cereal, chocolate chips, sugar and cocoa powder and mix well. Set aside.

Melt the almond butter, coconut oil, rice syrup, almond milk and vanilla in a small saucepan or pot set over a medium heat. Pour over the oat mixture and mix well so all the ingredients are well-coated.

Pour the bar mixture into the prepared baking pan and bake in the preheated oven for 30 minutes. Remove from the oven and set aside to cool completely before cutting into equal bars.

You don't need butter and eggs to make a delicious cookie with oats. These are vegan and I use coconut oil (my personal favourite) along with coconut sugar, which is low in glycemic sugar and gives an amazing flavour to drop cookies. While the Oatmeal Cranberry Cookies on page 48 are soft and chewy, these cookies are for those that like a little crispiness with each bite.

vegan chocolate chip cookies

125 ml/^{1}/2 cup coconut oil

100 g/^{1}/2 cup coconut sugar

150 g/1 ^{1}/2 cups old-fashioned rolled oats

100 g/^{3}/4 cup plain/all-purpose flour (plus ^{1}/2 teaspoon xanthan gum if using gluten-free plain/all-purpose flour)

^{1}/2 teaspoon bicarbonate of/baking soda

a pinch of salt

30 ml/^{1}/8 cup soy milk

80 g/^{1}/2 cup mini milk/semisweet chocolate chips

1 teaspoon pure vanilla extract

a baking sheet, greased and lined with baking parchment

Makes 12

Melt the coconut oil in a saucepan or pot set over a low heat. Pour the melted oil into a large mixing bowl and add the coconut sugar. Mix well, then add the oats, flour, bicarbonate of/baking soda and a pinch of salt. Mix again, then add the remaining ingredients. Stir, cover and set in the fridge to chill for 30 minutes.

Preheat the oven to 180°C (350°F) Gas 4.

Put a tablespoon of chilled dough onto the prepared baking sheet and press down slightly with your thumb. Bake the cookies in the preheated oven for 10–12 minutes.

Remove the cookies from the oven and set aside to cool for 15 minutes before transferring to a wire rack to cool completely and to prevent them from crumbling.

Oatmeal cookies are a classic treat and make a great gift wrapped in tissue paper and stored in a cookie jar. They are chewy, comforting and satisfying – they certainly won't last anywhere long.

oatmeal cranberry cookies

113 g/^{1}/2 cup butter (or melted coconut oil)

150 g/^{3}/4 cup dark brown sugar

1 egg

1 teaspoon pure vanilla extract

70 ml/^{1}/4 cup apple purée/sauce

135 g/1 ^{1}/8 cups plain/all-purpose flour (plus ^{1}/2 teaspoon xanthan gum if using gluten-free plain/all-purpose flour)

175 g/1 ^{3}/4 cups old-fashioned rolled oats

1 teaspoon bicarbonate of/baking soda

60 g/^{1}/2 cup dried cranberries

2 baking sheets, greased and lined with baking parchment

Makes 24

Preheat the oven to 180°C (350°F) Gas 4.

Cream the butter and sugar together in a large mixing bowl. It is easiest to do this by beating them together with an electric mixer until soft and creamy. Add the egg, vanilla, xanthan gum (if using) and apple purée/sauce and mix together until smooth.

In a separate bowl, whisk together the flour, oats and bicarbonate of/baking soda.

Add the dry mixture into the wet a little at a time until all the ingredients are well-coated. Finally, fold in the dried cranberries.

Put a tablespoon of chilled dough onto the prepared baking sheet and press down slightly with your thumb. Bake the cookies in the preheated oven for 12 minutes, or until the sides of the cookies are a toasty brown colour.

Remove the cookies from the oven and set aside to cool before serving.

This is a gooey, chewy cluster of goodness. The clusters are a sweet snack, perfect for a dessert bite or an indulgent on-the-go treat.

cocoa marshmallow oat clusters

150 g/1 $\frac{1}{2}$ cups old-fashioned
   rolled oats
75 g/$\frac{1}{4}$ cup almond butter
2 egg whites
4 tablespoons cocoa powder
2 tablespoons butter, melted
60 ml/$\frac{1}{4}$ cup honey
45 g/$\frac{3}{4}$ cup mini
   marshmallows
40 g/$\frac{1}{4}$ cup mini milk/
   semisweet chocolate chips
1 teaspoon pure vanilla
   extract
a pinch of salt

2 baking sheets, greased and
   lined with baking parchment

Makes 14

Preheat the oven to 180°C (350°F) Gas 4.

Spread the oats onto a baking sheet and toast in the preheated oven for about 15 minutes, or until golden. Remove from the oven and set aside to cool, keeping the oven on.

In a medium bowl, mix together the almond butter, egg whites, cocoa powder, butter and honey. Whisk until combined, then add the cooled toasted oats and mix again. Fold in the marshmallows and chocolate chips before adding the vanilla and a pinch of salt. Cover and set in the fridge to chill for 1 hour.

Put a tablespoon of chilled dough onto the prepared baking sheet and press down slightly with your thumb. Bake the cookies in the preheated oven for 12 minutes.

Remove the cookies from the oven and set aside to cool before serving.

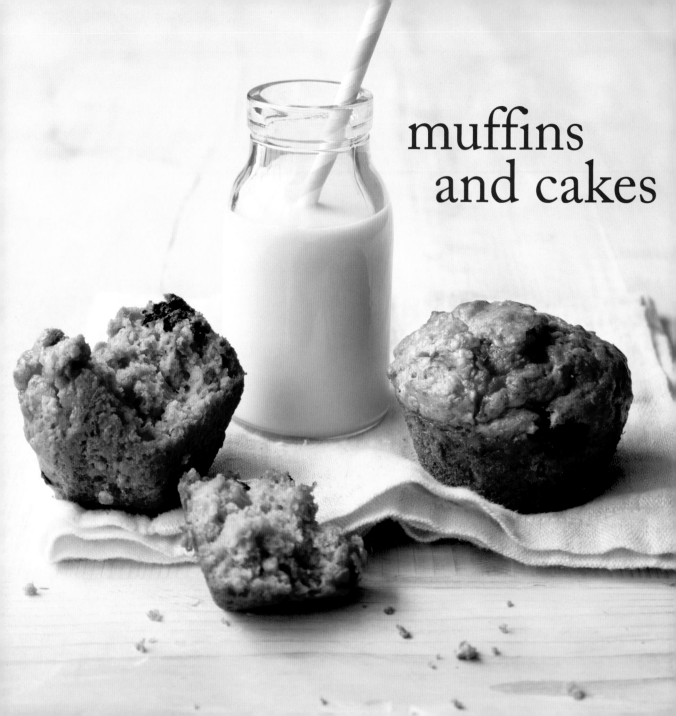

muffins
and cakes

If I was being treated to breakfast in bed, this is the muffin I would want to wake up to. I love the texture of oats within a morning muffin – they feel hearty. Oat flour is a great alternative to plain/all-purpose flour and works really well as a substitution for other flours in baked goods.

fruit and oat muffins

Fruit purée
150 ml/²/₃ cup soy milk
110 g/¹/₃ cup puréed figs (about 5)
80 g/¹/₃ cup pineapple pieces

Muffins
100 g/1 cup old-fashioned rolled oats
90 g/²/₃ cup oat flour
100 g/³/₄ cup plain/all-purpose flour (plus ¹/₂ teaspoon xanthan gum if using gluten-free plain/all-purpose flour)
110 g/¹/₂ cup brown sugar
1 teaspoon baking powder
1 teaspoon bicarbonate of/baking soda
¹/₂ teaspoon salt
2 eggs
1 teaspoon pure vanilla extract
100 ml/¹/₃ cup vegetable oil
100 g/1 cup fresh or frozen mixed berries

a 12-hole muffin pan, greased

Makes 12

Begin by making the fruit purée. Put 60 ml/¹/₄ cup of warm water, the soy milk, puréed figs and pineapple in a food processor and blend to a thick consistency. Set aside.

Preheat the oven to 180°C (350°F) Gas 4.

Mix together the oats, flours, sugar, baking powder, bicarbonate of/baking soda and salt in a large mixing bowl. In a separate bowl, mix together the prepared fruit purée, eggs, xanthan gum (if using) vanilla and oil. Add the dry mixture into the wet a little at a time before folding in the mixed berries.

Pour the batter into the prepared muffin pan and bake in the preheated oven for 20 minutes, or until a knife comes out clean. Remove from the oven and set aside to cool before serving.

This is a delightful cake for afternoon tea. Light, fluffy and moist, it is delicious served with a little plain yogurt on the side.

orange and cranberry tea cake

115 g/1 stick butter (at room temperature)

165 g/³/4 cup brown sugar

2 eggs

80 g/¹/3 cup plain yogurt, plus extra to serve

freshly squeezed juice and grated zest of 1 orange

1 teaspoon pure vanilla extract

100 g/1 cup plain/all-purpose flour (plus 1 teaspoon xanthan gum if using gluten-free plain/all-purpose flour)

35 g/¹/4 cup oat flour

35 g/¹/3 cup old-fashioned rolled oats

1 teaspoon bicarbonate of/baking soda

1 teaspoon baking powder

a pinch of salt

35 g/¹/3 cup fresh or frozen cranberries

a 23 x 12-cm/9 x 5-in loaf pan

Makes 8 slices

Preheat the oven to 180°C (350°F) Gas 4.

Cream the butter and sugar together in a large mixing bowl. It is easiest to do this by beating them together with an electric mixer until soft and creamy. Add the eggs, yogurt, xanthan gum (if using), orange juice and zest and vanilla.

Sift the flours into a separate bowl, add the oats, bicarbonate of/baking soda, baking powder and a pinch of salt, then stir. Beat the butter mixture into the flours before folding in the cranberries.

Pour the batter into the prepared loaf pan and bake in the preheated oven for 35–40 minutes, or until a knife comes out clean.

Remove from the oven and turn out onto a wire rack to cool before serving in slices with yogurt.

140 g/1 cup dry Date and
  Sunflower Muesli (see
  page 27)
70 g/^{1}/2 cup oat flour
30 g/^{1}/4 cup plain/all-purpose
  flour (plus ^{1}/2 teaspoon
  xanthan gum if using
  gluten-free plain/all-
  purpose flour)
60 g/^{1}/4 cup plain yogurt
200 ml/^{3}/4 cup almond milk
1 egg
115 ml/^{1}/3 cup maple syrup
1 teaspoon pure vanilla
  extract
1 teaspoon baking powder
1 teaspoon bicarbonate of/
  baking soda
a pinch of salt

a 12-hole muffin pan, greased
  and lined with 9 muffin cases

Makes 9

Muffins don't have to be an unhealthy choice for breakfast. Like anything else, it's all about what you put in them and there are so many options. A simplified muesli forms the base of this recipe. When you break the muffin apart, you see the delicious combination of oats, raisins and nuts, which are always a great start to the day.

muesli breakfast muffins

Put the muesli, flours, yogurt and milk in a large mixing bowl. Mix well, cover and set in the fridge to soak overnight.

The next morning, preheat the oven to 180°C (350°F) Gas 4.

In a separate bowl, mix the egg, maple syrup and vanilla together. Add to the soaked muesli mixture and stir well. Add the baking powder, bicarbonate of/baking soda, xanthan gum (if using) and a pinch of salt before pouring the batter into the prepared muffin pan.

Bake in the preheated oven for 20–25 minutes, or until a knife comes out clean. Remove from the oven and set on a wire rack to cool before serving.

A good carrot cake is hard to beat. I love taking a dessert and transforming it slightly so it doesn't feel like such a guilty pleasure.

carrot oat squares

150 g/1¹/4 cups plain/all-
  purpose flour (plus
  1 teaspoon xanthan gum
  if using gluten-free plain/
  all-purpose flour)
100 g/1 cup old-fashioned
  rolled oats
110 g/¹/2 cup brown sugar
1 teaspoon bicarbonate of/
  baking soda
¹/2 teaspoon baking powder
1 teaspoon ground cinnamon
¹/2 teaspoon ground nutmeg
a pinch of salt
25 g/¹/4 cup chopped walnuts
35 g/¹/4 cup (dark) raisins
115 g/¹/3 cup butter, melted
1 egg
210 ml/³/4 cup apple purée/
  sauce
¹/2 teaspoon pure vanilla
  extract
4 medium carrots, grated

a 20 x 28-cm/8 x 11-in baking
  pan, greased

Makes 10

Preheat the oven to 180°C (350°F) Gas 4.

Mix together the flour, oats, sugar, bicarbonate of/baking soda, baking powder, cinnamon, nutmeg and salt in a large mixing bowl. Add the walnuts and raisins and set aside.

In a separate bowl whisk together the xanthan gum (if using), melted butter, egg, apple purée/sauce and vanilla. Stir in the grated carrots, then mix the wet mixture into the dry.

Pour the batter into the prepared baking pan and bake in the preheated oven for 30 minutes, or until a knife comes out clean. Remove from the oven and set aside to cool completely before cutting into equal squares.

smoothies

The beautiful thing about frozen fruit is that you can bring any season to the table. These are great summer drinks. Make your own milk using oats as a dairy- and nut-free alternative!

peach chia oat smoothie

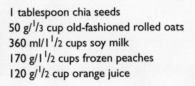

1 tablespoon chia seeds
50 g/⅓ cup old-fashioned rolled oats
360 ml/1½ cups soy milk
170 g/1½ cups frozen peaches
120 g/½ cup orange juice

1 teaspoon pure vanilla extract
1 teaspoon ground cinnamon
1 tablespoon honey

Serves 2

Soak the chia seeds in 4 tablespoons of water, cover and chill in the fridge for at least an hour, stirring after 10 minutes. Meanwhile, soak the oats in the soy milk, cover and chill in the fridge for 20 minutes, until the oats are soft.

When the chia seeds and oats are ready, put all of the ingredients in a food processor and blend to a smooth consistency. Serve immediately.

cocoa oat smoothie

100 g/1 cup steel-cut oats
1 small banana
1½ tablespoons cocoa powder
½ teaspoon pure vanilla extract
2 fresh figs

2 tablespoons honey
170g/1 cup ice

Serves 2

Cover the oats with water and leave to soak for at least 30 minutes, or up to 12 hours. Rinse and drain the oats in a sieve/strainer. Put them in a food processor with 750 ml/3 cups of water and blend. Strain the resulting milk using a fine mesh sieve/strainer set over a jug/pitcher, then strain again.

Pour the 360 ml/1½ cups of the oat milk into a food processor with the other ingredients and blend until smooth. Serve immediately.

35 g/⅓ cup old-fashioned
    rolled oats
360 ml/1½ cups almond milk
1 banana
4 tablespoons peanut butter
2 tablespoons agave syrup
170 g/1 cup ice

Serves 2

This is a very hearty and satisfying breakfast or the perfect pre-exercise boost. It can be made using any nut butter that you have to hand, so pick your favourite to get you going.

peanut butter oat smoothie

Soak the oats in the almond milk, cover and chill in the fridge for 20 minutes, until the oats are soft.

When the oats are ready, put all of the ingredients in a food processor and blend to a smooth consistency. Serve immediately.

35 g/⅓ cup old-fashioned
    rolled oats
360 ml/1½ cups almond milk
130 g/1 cup frozen mixed
    berries
120 g/½ cup plain yogurt
2 tablespoons honey
75 g/⅓ cup ice

Serves 2

The perfect on-the-go breakfast, I love the purple colour that blueberries give to this drink. Even better – it tastes just as good as it looks!

blueberry oat smoothie

Soak the oats in the almond milk, cover and chill in the fridge for 20 minutes, until the oats are soft.

When the oats are ready, put all of the ingredients in a food processor and blend to a smooth consistency. Serve immediately.

index